Letter to 'Oumuamua

Letter to 'Oumuamua

JAMES NORCLIFFE

OTAGO UNIVERSITY PRESS
Te Whare Tā o Te Wānanga o Ōtākou

For Elizabeth and Alejandro

CONTENTS

FOUR
Letters

Letter to 'Oumuamua

Dear 'Oumuamua

This morning I saw a willow tree in first-spring,
flush of green in a paddock full of black, sleeping steers.

It was a prayer in the still air, morning sun and the sea beyond;
nothing to make the new leaves quiver except celebration.

I note you didn't hang around, dear 'Oumuamua: one brief
look was all it took before you hoisted your great light sail

and hightailed it out of here. I understand your misgivings,
'Oumuamua. I have them, too. But it's, we're, not all bad really.

A kind farmer allowed this willow to live, give shelter to his cattle
as they wait for the abattoir. That has to be worth something, doesn't it?

And from this distance the sea is blue and apparently cold, the hills
almost green, the cattle innocent, and the willow celebrating.

I'm not saying come back, dear 'Oumuamua, we do know what
we're doing. We're not all bad. We just can't help ourselves.

DEAR VALUED CUSTOMER

We acknowledge receipt of your recent order for one (1) Glorious Morning™.

Please note that because of unexpectedly high demand, shipping difficulties and the vagaries of the postal service at present, delivery of this item may be delayed rather longer than we would like.

It is our company's policy to market only the highest quality merchandise and you will note from customer reviews that the item you have chosen one (1) Glorious Morning™ comes highly recommended, with the large majority of purchasers expressing full satisfaction by awarding the product five stars.

We are convinced that you will not be disappointed with your decision once you receive it.

We crave your patience given that at present Glorious Morning™ is in such short supply. Please don't be tempted to pivot to a cheaper product which, while it may be more available, will not guarantee lasting satisfaction. Such alternatives may provide a brief period of glory but component failure or an inferior battery will return you to your current forlorn world after an hour or so.

We do appreciate how frustrating it must be to suffer the long succession of shitty mornings you are currently experiencing and why you must be so looking forward to the delivery of your order.

We can only say be patient. We have placed your order, we acknowledge your payment, but the rest is really out of our hands.

All that is in our power at our end we have done.

Trust us.

Dear Contributor

Spruce is a member of the *Picea* family. It is a coniferous evergreen from the northern temperate and boreal regions of the earth.

Pine trees are also conifers, also evergreen, and comprise members of the very large *Pinus* family.

Larch is another conifer of the genus *Larix* from the boreal regions of the earth. It differs from the aforementioned in that it is deciduous.

Hemlock is yet another conifer, a member of the *Tsuga* family, found in North America and parts of Asia. It is not to be confused with the herb hemlock, a decoction of which was used to put Socrates to death.

The above are all useful and beautiful trees, none of which we are prepared to sacrifice in order to publish your contribution.

Sincerely

The Editors

DEAR KERERŪ

Etched black against
a deep blue sky, your
wings are outstretched
like a Habsburg eagle.

Who do you think
you're fooling, you silly,
playing against type –
when your true role is

swaying on a wobbly
power line, your bright
white breast plumped
with apprehension,

or bouncing on a tree
lucerne's branches far
too slender for your
weight and security?

But it's all a double
bluff. Your tomfoolery
is just another act
isn't it, dear Kererū?

For when you launch
from tree to tree your
clatter belies your miracle
doesn't it, dear Kererū?

As your clatter, my darling,
and mine, our clatter,
belies our miracle, too.

The Museum of
UNNATURAL HISTORY

5.02 FROM ST PANCRAS

So tired, gripping the pole, chin resting on the back of my hand; a voice and another voice discuss a dinner, then the possibility of another perhaps, sometime, next time she's up in Oxford.

A woman switches off her phone, reaches into her handbag for a book.

In the dark window a man with his head on his hand stares at me over the hand for an unfamiliar moment.

The book is about grief. There is a long passage in italics I cannot read but the woman can. She has almost finished the book, but had preferred her phone.

I can understand that. The man in the dark window has raised his head from his hand. He stares expressionlessly.

The first voice speaks too loudly and too quickly. He reveals much but seems not to care.

The woman leaves the italics and turns to the supplement at the back of the book. Titles are in bold. The supplement lists helpful organisations for those whom suicide has visited or is about to visit.

The second voice is soft, directed towards the first voice.

Samaritans. Papyrus. The Lives Left Behind.

The face in the window looks away.

The woman returns the book to her bag, retrieves her phone and turns it on.

There is laughter. That would be nice, the second voice says.

Art and confusion

You step into a picture palace and into a different light.

The woman you are with stops just beyond the top of the stairs to answer her phone. She is moving away from you, leaving you.

There are large, framed posters announcing forthcoming movies of manufactured wars, lives and loves. There are other large posters announcing caricatures of these.

The light is the colour of glass, the colour of pinot gris. People move back and forth sipping at the light from short-stemmed glasses. They stand beneath the posters, their faces tiny beneath the faces in the posters.

The woman you are with is still speaking on her phone. She does not look around. She does not look anywhere.

The posters obey the laws of perspective, but not of time, truth or colour. This does not seem to offend the people moving back and forth and you wonder why.

You buy two glasses of pinot gris at the bar and carry them to the woman you are with, still talking on her phone. She senses you there and reaches for one. She nods thank you but does not look at you. You sip at the light, wondering when she will return.

You are in, you realise suddenly, a scene from a movie, a scene that must feature on a poster somewhere and you look around the walls again.

The woman you are with does not have this realisation. She presses her tiny face to her phone, unaware of the walls, the posters, the movie she is in, even as the bells begin to ring.

PINK ASPIRIN FOR THE HEART

Have you any aspirin for the heart?
Small pills, pink and heart-shaped:
this being an unfunny pharmaceutical
joke, an exercise in metonymy,
synecdoche, one or the other, or both.

Blood sometimes trickles thickly
when it ought to flow more quickly
like the water it is considered thicker
than. It should flow like a gazelle
through graceful grass, like cursive

script across the smoothness
of bond paper looping in curves, in
curlicues of red. Mine doesn't always.
It sticks, stodges, clogs and needs
this irony of pink aspirin to free it up.

But in our blood-soaked age, blood
should be thicker, surely; should
staunch and seal itself defiantly in
clots and scabs. The gazelle should
rest beneath the willow, the script

should pause, reflect; consider capital
letters better to clump and thump;
consider pen and sword; that blood
should not flood arenas and mosques;
that there should be another pill for that.

THEN DR SALK

The facts: a boy with red hair, violent, easily brought to rage; fists and blood-rush.

Choirs surround him; anthems of lust.

The visit: then Dr Salk came with his vulcanite suitcases, towers of waxed paper cups, flasks of pink emulsion.

The conceit: a line of willows bent yellow over the stream like frozen dancers: a Salk vaccine protecting the grass from frost.

The aftermath: the staff take the boy away. The rabble forms a line. We raise our paper cups, down the emulsion; drown the noise, the baying, the fear of callipers.

The toast: we drink to the good, self-denying doctor, to the end of winter, of frost, to the end of violence, drink deeply of sweetness, pinkness, health.

RAGE

After the roaring stopped, the gasping stopped,
and then the coughing, and the hiccoughing.
They all stopped. And then there was silence.

He rubbed at his wet face and smeared his cheeks.
He opened his eyes. He looked about him in that silence.
The room was empty. He had driven them away:

his soft mama, his papa, his confused grandparents,
his little brother in his carrycot. All were gone.
As were the red sofa, the easy chair, the electric piano.

The table and the dining chairs. The painting on the wall
of the distant mountain. The low table scattered with
his books and the cabinet where he kept his toys. All gone.

The curtains had disappeared and the sun was low
in the west. The light crept across the carpet,
leaving him, making silently for the window.

3 A.M.

You wake slippery with sweat in the night
listening hard for what *danse macabre* might
have brought you to this pitch of attention:
perhaps the beep of a truck travelling backwards.

You sense syncopation and there are voices
too, whispering with a hint of talcum, there is
foot-tapping jazz, and an all but tuneless humming
with only the words of a chorus half-remembered.

You draw apart your heavy drapes as if drawing
the curtains of a stage but there is no combo
performing on the footpath, only the sodium light
at the corner, static, not tracking for a lucky spot.

But somewhere beyond darkness there are faceless
figures waiting, with arms stretched, waists held,
readying themselves for a lambada to impossible
music and spangled under a mirror ball of stars.

Insomnia

The night becomes long for you. The curtains are not able to shut out the night or the tumbling. The counterpane with its stylised trees becomes a provocation, mocking your purpose.

And so begins the endless debate about directions and whether this path or that path through the storied suburbs of the past would have been better. This followed by the debate about whether the debate itself has any point.

You had chosen the path that has led to this night. You preferred wet leaves to bitumen. You had paused because of the pigeon with the broken wing, the lost child, the weeping woman, the man who made you laugh.

That path is no more real now than the trees on the bed. The pigeon recovered and flew away. The child was found and lost and found again. The woman died. The man makes you laugh and makes you weep and makes you laugh.

He makes you weep and makes you laugh and makes you weep, but nothing can make you sleep.

A DAY LIKE NO OTHER

Through the swirl of the dust and the smoke of the past, you can hear again the furious clicking of an abacus.

Spring has infected the pigeons, driven them mad. They scramble through the leaves to get close and they scramble through the leaves to get far away.

The plumbers have brought jackhammers into the living room. They are large determined men. The pipes are not safe.

We have received news about the little cat. It is not good.

The Notre Dame is burning.

Christchurch has a new meaning.

We must leave the house before the incessant clicking, the smoke, and the dust become completely unbearable.

We struggle to hold on to this knowledge.

But it is too late. The incessant clicking, the smoke, and the dust have already become completely unbearable.

THE MUSEUM OF UNNATURAL HISTORY

can be seen through the mist at certain times of the day
on the danger side of the yellow line at the station platform.

Beyond the rails there are deserted streets where
deserted houses lean drunkenly against each other.

The last newspaper, driven by a gritty wind, flaps
down a road. The banner headline is obscured.

Ice falls from the trees like white petals and
the great, bare branches reach up struggling with

the memory of birds. The wind picks up, colder now,
lifting the paper. You'd almost think it was alive.

LOOKING FOR NOVELS SET IN VIENNA

The mirrors must be covered, the old lady said. It is the custom.
Black crepe is advised, but anything will do; even white calico.
The dead must not be allowed to seize their opportunity.

How soon they change, as they must. Their needs are different
now, as ours are. Leave the house, I tell you, leave the house.
Make your way to the park by the canal. With the mirrors covered,

I assure you, you will not be followed. Find the carousel and let
the Wurlitzer drown your heartbeat. Climb on to a white horse
and grip the pole. The mirrors will be covered. The horse will take

you round and round and up and down. There will be a period
of mourning. Grip the pole. Wait for the stars. They will come.

SCANDINAVIAN NOIR

Before the murder

Their phones are silent.
There are no sirens yet.

The cat in the alley does
not look about or run.

The window is grimy;
he rubs at it with his elbow.

At times like this, he thinks,
every room is a waiting room.

She is puzzling over
the answer to sixteen across.

He looks up at
the clock on the wall.

The cars slick down
the commuter highway

and over the bridge,
red taillights, indicators.

Seconds, minutes, hours;
the anxious darkness.

After the murder

The detective whose dark intensity is hidden beneath a layer of dark intensity stares at the horizon.

Her partner whose dark intensity is hidden beneath a layer of jaunty insouciance picks his teeth.

All day it has rained, testing their patience and the windscreen wipers, muddying the evidence.

The witnesses who had seen little had said a lot; the witnesses who had seen a lot had said little.

After the murder everything is utterly unchanged, yet utterly different. The sky is grey but should be green.

All appears empty and there is a line where the world falls away and beyond the line the endless invisible sea.

She stares at the horizon wishing for the wisdom of the moment. Her partner picks his teeth.

THE MAN WHO TURNED HIMSELF
INTO A GUN

At first he thought bullets;
then he expressed them.

He became gun-metal grey,
cold to the touch.

He wanted to press himself
into evil's shoulder, be cradled there.

He wanted to be trained in evil's grip,
evil's telescopic sight in his sight.

Above all he wanted evil's finger feeling for,
feathering, depressing his progressive trigger.

He was sleek, he was balanced:
no longer flesh, no longer sentient,

weighted,
then weightless

mechanically perfect,
perfectly mechanical.

WE COME EASILY TO THE LANGUAGE OF HORROR

Ramshackle, your dilapidated house of lies. Your method so insidious:
say something perverse and call it wisdom. Your piles lean drunkenly,
your soffits rotten, your lath and plaster held together by scrim. Then
go to the market, find a beautiful bowl, hand-crafted, salt-glazed, as
glassy-green as envy. Place it on a polished table. Walnut. Cabriole legs.
Silk crocheted doily. Fill the bowl with clear water and daffodils, bright
yellow trumpets singing of spring. Their perfume will smother the stench
of corruption, the leaky cistern, the foul drains. Don't call it perverse: call
it wisdom. See, it works.

The search party

When the search party was formed, of course I volunteered. It was expected and I had the necessary skills and equipment: curiosity, eyes and legs.

Just as we packed up, so did the weather. The sky lowered and there was a deep fog, reducing all visibility and turning our torches against us.

This increased the importance of our whistles. At the same time, the fog disrupted the sonic pattern so that while we could hear the blasts, their direction eluded us.

The dogs were useless. Once unleashed, they raced through the murk barking furiously but pointlessly. The lost whistles coming from all points of the compass seemed to goad them into a greater frenzy. The torches confused them.

We had been told to keep to the pathways once we entered the forest. However, the fog blanked out all evidence of the pathways, even the pathway into the forest itself.

Our being in the forest was only revealed tree by tree as we reached and discovered the Braille of hammered bark and tall, darker shapes directly in front of us, blocking our way.

I say 'we' and 'us' advisedly, for I soon became separated from my companions and they from theirs.

I could have panicked at this point and sought to find my fellow searchers, but I was of a phlegmatic disposition and I had to try to keep in mind the greater goal, although this was difficult as the briefing, beyond issuing our torches and whistles, had never quite made that greater goal clear.

Light the log burner. Let trees burn,
words burn. Keep yourself warm
this cold night. Open the damper.

The fire will roar. Draw the curtain
on the scarlet sky. Darkness is not
far away and neither is the frost.

Let the deceased descend from the shelf
and disport themselves on the table
beside a pot of freshly brewed coffee.

The letters form themselves into names
you know well but cannot really
know at all. Let them announce themselves.

Here we are, they whisper. Here we are
again. The same as we always were, but
different – as of course you are, dear reader.

You must forgive us for reminding you
of this. We cannot help being dog-eared,
fly-spotted and ever so slightly foxed

as you are, dear reader, as you are, even as
the fire goes out and the coffee grows cold.

THE SONG OF THE FOREST AT MARSHALSWICK

is constrained contained behind wire and iron gates
plane trees oak trees lime trees holly
melancholy

arms elbows limbs trimmed to reach stretch and shoulder
holly trees plane trees oak trees lime
lost in time

history of wind thinned by weather by season
lime trees plane trees holly trees oak
creak and croak

the forest charter started well ended with treason
oak trees lime trees holly trees plane
wind and rain

bramble dock nettle settle edgily and sprawly
plane trees oak trees lime trees holly:
human folly

WOLF LIGHT

L'heure entre chien et loup

1

Wolf light: between your
out-breath and your in-breath;
your in-breath and your out-breath,
the stasis mimicking the real thing.

2

The time of fading
bees and dying ladybirds.

When the drone of distant motorways
drowns chittering and buzz:
the grey time where
all noise becomes white.

3

The little ones bring us stories.
They want us to read to them,
to embroider the bright illustrations
and make them even brighter.

How can we resist?
Lying is in our blood.

4

Buzz, drone, lies
and wolf light and after
wolf light: darkness.
After darkness: darkness.

Hoopsa boyaboy hoopsa!

after Antonio Vivaldi

1 *L'inverno*

Here is the red priest. He is racing across the Rialto with fiddles galloping furioso in his head, at his heels.

Here are the girls in the orphanage waiting. It is cold. One, the favoured one, blows a pitch pipe. The others, the less favoured ones, form their mouths into perfect o's. They blow practice notes through their mouths like perfect bubbles, finding their perfect pitch.

There is percussion in the cobblestones. The red priest loves the regularity of it. It is a beat he favours. His feet find his perfect beat.

The freezing wind off the sea is channelled along the canals. The red priest does not feel the cold. He has found his beat. He has his hoop, his whoop de boop. It rolls beside him.

2 *La primavera*

Listen to the shepherds! The prance of lambs, pan pipes dancing with spring, with quickening, with wombfruit, with bags and bagpipes! O perfect o's, O Arcady, the cuckoo sleeping in the nest and the red-headed priest taking notes. But a thickening, quickening sky darkens.

Thunderclouds, Spring's midwives, allegro non molto, arriving apace. The shepherds look up, the red priest looks up, casts his notebook aside and hurries back to the orphanage, a spring in his step.

3 L'estate

Too hot for effort, too hot even to swat the drowsy mosquitoes, dry wind
in his airs, ruffling his red hair, the red priest lolls. O boy, o boyaboy.
The boatman leaning on his pole, pushing past pigeon-stained palazzi,
past basilica and campanile towards the Pio Ospedale della Pietà and the
nuns, the choirgirls, the violins. O boy. O turtle doves. O whipped cream
of cumulonimbus. O thunder.

4 L'autunno

Horns and baying hounds, the gust of hunters disappear over the hill,
tallyhoing the undergrowth for the fox, the hare, for whatever's there to
shoot, the pursuit that drives them onward, searching.

The red priest too is driven onward, the grey-gowned girls file silent,
adagio molto, into the capella.

Here is the favoured one fingering her pitch pipe, here the less favoured
ones wait in lines. Red leaves are falling, swallows leaving, the red priest
blots his pages after blowing on the ink.

His wig awry the red priest labours. The girls wait. The forthbringing
almost done, furioso, his quill quivers. O boyaboy, the red priest
whispers.

Mares' tails, curly hooks, race. There will be rain. The sound of horns. A
fleeing beast, a pursuit almost caught.

The quickening. His smile. She puts the pitch pipe to her mouth.

Really
HOT SOUP

LIVING IN THE ENTROPICS

Short days, sharp days, long nights come on apace.
Ah, who shall hide us from the winter's face?
Cold doth increase, the sickness will not cease,
And here we lie, God knows, with little ease.
    From winter, plague, & pestilence, good Lord, deliver us!
                                    —THOMAS NASHE, FROM 'AUTUMN'

We love it here,
on our entropical island

even though the leaves are brown and shrivelled
in the unreasonable, unseasonable frosts.

We used to walk in the city
until our soles fell away,

and now we hear the city itself
has fallen away.

Still, we love it here on our island
despite its growing smaller as the tides encroach.

Luckily, we can no longer see the tides;
in fact, we can no longer see the sea

because our hedges have grown so high
since our shears disintegrated and our ladder collapsed.

We don't really worry about the ladder –
it was getting hard to climb anyway

and the shears were blunt
and increasingly stiff and hard to grip.

Also, we rather like the height of the hedges
although, as noted, their leaves have shrivelled in these weird frosts.

There is talk of a disease. Another one.
There is always talk of another disease.

It is said that love, though, is erosion free,
that love survives all.

We don't know if that is true.
We don't know if anything is true,

but part of us wants to believe it.

LAMBTON QUAY

Life is so complicated today, she says,
troubled by the ethics of pet food:
whether it should or should not contain
corn starch, soybean meal and rice bran,
cattle bones and chicken feathers,
whether our much-loved Sammy
should only eat much-loved cows, hens and pigs;

not thinking of, or troubled at all by, the plight
of the juggler who has lost every last one
of his coloured balls attempting the impossible
on Lambton Quay – an ambitious dream
which completely stuffed his revenue stream;
nor even worried about Lambton Quay,
that the sea is returning to the land
that the land is returning to the sea.

Ocean View

Sea breeze, land breeze
here where the world breathes
and the tide is running.

See Granddad with his
knotted handkerchief,
his trousers rolled,

still carrying his bucket
and spade, the sea
roiling about his ankles.

All of his sandcastles
washing away, washing
away like sandcastles.

Foam and spume
have flecked and bleared
his glasses, the waves

have seized his teeth.
Land breeze, sea breeze,
and the tide is running

and Granddad's running
and Grandma's running
from the world's breath.

Really hot soup

Really hot soup is a change in the statistical distribution of soup patterns when that change lasts for an extended period of time (i.e., decades to millions of years). Really hot soup may refer to a change in average soup conditions, or in the time variation of soup within the context of longer-term average conditions.

Warmer soup is caused by factors such as calorific processes, variations in hot plate conditions received by plate tectonics, and volcanic over-flowing. Certain human activities have been identified as primary causes of ongoing really hot soup, often referred to as over-spicing.

Scientists actively work to understand past and future soup conditions by using observations and theoretical models. A culinary record – extending deep into the kitchen's past – has been put together, and continues to be built up, based on evidence of hotplate temperature profiles, bench-top stains and other analyses of soup layers, and records of past warm soup levels.

More recent data are provided by the instrumental record. Future patterns of potentially really, really hot soup, based on the physical sciences, are often used in theoretical approaches to match past warm soup data, make future projections, and link causes and effects of catastrophically hot soup.

This is an ongoing situation and potentially a very, very serious one, but there appears to be no easy solution.

People seem not to appreciate the very real dangers of really hot soup, not even when they're in it.

LIVING IN THE GOLDILOCKS ZONE

We used to enjoy living here.
There were quince trees
and apricots trees blossoming
in our garden. Life was nice.

The lawns were neatly trimmed
and the edges contained.
In the distance was a pleasant
view of a well-behaved ocean.

Of course there was that
ramshackle bach deep in
the woods where the bears lived.
But it was easy to avoid.

We just didn't go there,
preferring our raised beds,
and the exemplary manners
of beans, carrots and broccoli.

Life, as I said, was nice:
we lived within careful
parameters and had
circumscribed extremes.

We used to enjoy living here
on our pretty little planet.
Porridge was always provided
at the designated time.

But now the lawns are brown,
as dry and crunchy
underfoot as cornflakes;
the carrots droop and shrivel.

And all the bowls: little,
middle-sized and extra large
are much, much too hot to touch
and every bear is angry.

Kōtuku

It isn't rain, just a heavy mist
preferable to the relentless sun
of the last few days: the wilting leaves
like prayer flags drooping in the windless
heat, the baked grass white and crunchy.
Some relief, I guess, not that it will
last. Then a corner, then the curve
of the road, a dark ellipse beside
the sea, and standing ankle-deep
two white herons together stabbing
at the water. How white they are
in a grey world. One lifts its head and
looks up as I drive past. How white;
how beautiful; how far from the fires
up north. It is so very hard not
to sense reproach in that glance and I'm
grateful to turn into the mist once
more, thick mist, swirling like guilt.

Knowing what we are

It is dusk. Birds have gathered
on the shining mudflats.

Knowing what we are, they lift
into the air crying at our approach.

No economist can count them,
can estimate their scatter.

Any day soon, the birds will fly
far beyond the red-rimmed horizon.

Much later they will return. Neither
here nor there is home, yet both are.

Knowing what you are, I take your hand.
Neither here nor there, I try to count the days.

No economist can count them; neither
they nor we can estimate their scatter.

The coal range

1

When her man was killed in the mine,
her brothers moved my aunt from the hill
and built a house for her in the village.

In my house of memory there is a lean-to
back porch, with a washhouse and a lavatory,
a kitchen, a bathroom, and two bedrooms.

There is a lounge off the passage and a front door.
To one side of the veranda there is a sunroom
where her widowed father smokes his pipe.

On the kitchen floor was laid floral-patterned
Congoleum, bright before it cracked and faded,
and here and there a crocheted rag rug.

The enamelled Shacklock coal range dominates.
It is cream and green with a firebox to the left.
Two covered boxes sit on either side of the hearth,

one contains kindling and the other old magazines.
Each morning my aunt cleans out the grate. She takes
the ash and cinders away in a galvanised bucket.

Then she bunches newspaper into roses and builds
a raft of kindling on top. Finally, she places lumps
of coal on the kindling and sets the paper alight.

To get the fire burning sweetly she sometimes
needs to sugar the reluctant embers. In half an
hour the hotplates are ready for the porridge pot.

She, her father, and her little girl eat the porridge
with milk and salt, the Scottish way. She'd stirred
the pot clockwise, as always, to keep the de'il away.

2

Beyond the village there is a railway junction.
The main line heads up the coast, the branch
line heads into the hills and the mountains of coal.

Like blood, the coal runs in veins, and scabs
on the landscape. Coal pours down the hillside
through broadleaf and blackberry and is taken away.

The clank of wagons, gasp of loco, and drum of rain
drown the sound of the river running over rocks.
Nothing is soft, only the mist in the armpits of the hills.

3

The brothers every so often bring a truckload of coal
and dump it by the house: a small black mountain
my aunt mines with spade and scuttle to feed her stove.

The burning coal and smoke smell of Auld Reekie,
of far-away home. Pinned on the Pinex walls are
calendars: Scottie dogs, pipers and Greyfriars Bobby.

Sentiment sweetens distance, as drop scones, ANZAC
biscuits and peanut brownies sweeten the sour
pervading presence of damp coal, smoke and tea-tree.

4

Of course, her brothers have died, my aunt has died,
the village has died and the coal is dying. The blackberry
and honeysuckle grow wilder along the rusting railway lines

and the river, bolder now, races over rocks, ever more noisily.
In my house of memory, the coal range – long gone – sits
innocently, as a pan fries the last of the whitebait in fritters.

The
UNNATURAL
WORLD

Cow

He is learning language.
He points.

The table is a cow.
The plate is a cow.
The book is a cow.
The fridge magnet is a cow.
The fridge magnet is a picture of a cow.

And then I see I have it all wrong:

The cow is a table.
The cow is a plate.
The cow is a book.
The fridge magnet is a cow.

And he wants to tell Papa.
And he wants to tell Mama.
He is pointing at a table,
a plate and a book.
He is pointing at a cow
stuck on the fridge.
The cow is a fridge magnet
is a fridge magnet is a cow.

SAUERKRAUT

I worry about your cough. It comes on you unannounced
like some bore, some caller at the door who doesn't
get termination signals. These Indian summer days
we walk the hills, but choose our route more carefully.
The views are factored in of course: the sea through
pines, the line stretched between the heads, the high
horizon – and the gradient. We have to consider, too,
the wind. Our wind, not the pine-bending bough-
breaking kind, though that as well. One pace at a time:
take care of the steps so that the miles take care
of themselves; conserving ourselves, preserving, avoiding
pretty pickles, but still pressing the white cabbage
that will be sauerkraut into a bright green crock.

DUCK MOUSSE FOR BREAKFAST

such a morning
brilliance from the east
shining pink in the window

coffee in the pot
steam and happiness
then bread in the toaster

finally to peel a can
of force-fed canard all
the way from France, to spread

its pinkness over
buttered crispness
to bite to drink to bite

while the ducklings in a line
follow their mother
across the lawn, down

to the old mulberry tree
where they pick peck at berries
staining their little beaks red

FALCON

For days the dehumidifier
has sucked the water from our lives.
We have lived with its white roar,
its bleeps, gurgles and hot breath.

It is turning the concrete to sand,
us to dust. We haunt the sink
and the water jug as if they were oases,
and the windows were palm trees.

It's so good to escape back out into
the world of burst pipes and puddles,
to lie back on green grass and stare
up at the blue sea, the coral clouds

where birds are flocks of fish
the falcon a beautiful shark.

THE COMPLETE LACK OF EVIDENCE
IS PROOF THE CONSPIRACY IS WORKING

Cui bono, little bird
when I throw bread
on the lawn?

Even though you
can't see them, bird,
preoccupied

as you are with
the crumbs I scatter
before you,

there are larger
wings in the sky,
much larger

wings than yours
little bird,
watching, waiting,

and above those wings
even larger wings watching
smiling.

THE GOLDFISH

I did not like Gloria. I sensed her disapproval and responded in kind. She aspired to be the perfect hostess, so I was a particular challenge. Of course, she tried too hard. She tinkled too loudly at my one attempt at humour; she gazed around the table at the others as if encouraging them to laugh as well. It was patronising. It was hard not to feel diminished.

My response was to shrink into silence, avoiding all eye contact. I stared into my soup as if looking for a goldfish in its depths. That there was *something* lurking beneath the garnish of chopped cilantro seemed probable given the slight flurries of movement in the liquid, the popping of tiny bubbles on the surface. It may well have been a goldfish. Or a guppy. Perhaps, even, a baby turtle.

I pushed the bowl aside, unwilling to risk damaging the goldfish (or guppy) with my spoon, and certainly not willing to drain the bowl, thus exposing the fish to die a gasping death. I could imagine it flopping helplessly at the bottom. I could hear the astonished comments. Of course, there may not have been a goldfish in the bowl and, even if there were, it may not have been endangered.

However, it satisfied me to believe that there was a goldfish there. It gave me a more tangible reason to dislike Gloria, to say in response to her solicitous question that there was nothing wrong with the soup, nothing at all, and that I had enjoyed my few mouthfuls immensely.

Rabbits

His new scheme involved rabbits. He wanted to farm them. More correctly, he wished to farm softness. White softness: white softness with large red eyes.

He had a childhood memory of a small rabbit. A small sweet rabbit that died too young. The memory was probably false, but he wanted to make it real.

The small rabbit possibly had a name, but it was a name he had forgotten. Perhaps it was simply Rabbit. Like Woman. Man. Platypus.

He thought he would use the chicken model. This of course involved cages even though he would have preferred hutches. He liked the word hutch. It rhymed with crutch and he always considered crutches supportive.

Cages were also supportive and they would house rabbits more efficiently; any new enterprise demanded efficiency to get it off the ground.

The cages would be off the ground, too, and so, therefore, would be the rabbits. He felt, like chickens, they could be reduced to nuggets even though nuggets were crumbed and gold, not white, and nuggets were crunchy rather than soft.

She was not impressed. Why not chickens in that case? People could not tell the difference without a point of difference. What is the point?

Fun shapes, he said. Fun shapes would be the point of difference. The nuggets could be fun shapes. Tiny rabbits. Nuggets shaped like rabbits. Nuggets with tiny rabbit ears like the V for victory sign. Nuggets with small red eyes.

You could be on to something, she said.

Mr Fizz

We buried Mr Fizz today with all due rites and ceremonies as befitting one
with such a beautiful singing voice and one who insisted on doing things
his way. They say things unsaid, unsung, are sweeter, but don't believe
it. The silence was unnerving, all but frightening, when the memory of
melody was so near.

The obsequies were few and halting. Mr Fizz had been such a presence
in our lives that his sudden absence seemed to induce aphasia. He was …
someone began. I'd like to … another started. Nobody really knew how to
begin or, if started, had any idea how to continue and all attempts petered
out into incoherence.

Truth to tell, I believe we all understood as we stood around the dreadful
hole, how little we really knew of Mr Fizz. Was his faithful companion,
that faux-leopard-skin overnight bag, an expression of poverty or of
heightened irony.

Of his likes and dislikes we knew little. His visits were fleeting and his
conversation minimal. For all that, we understood a deep antipathy to
cats. This made the leopard-skin overnight bag doubly ambiguous and the
cause (later) of much speculation. So much, as with this dislike of cats, we
were forced to intuit. A sweet tooth? Probably. A love life?
Who knew?

To use an airport analogy, we found ourselves bereft, leaving the departure
lounge of an airport having said goodbye to Mr Fizz.

But then again, that was not right either. We *were* at an airport, but in
the arrivals lounge, or more correctly the Collect Baggage area. There
was a single item on the carousel: Mr Fizz's faux-leopard-skin overnight
bag. We stood in the unnerving silence as it went round and around
and around. The knowledge that Mr Fizz would never uplift it was
unbearably distressing.

GREENFINCHES AND WAX-EYES AMONG THE FIGS

Autumn's almost gone, but the fig tree
is green still, messy branches held up to the sun
still fattening its crop of finch-coloured figs

attracting the finches themselves
who arrive one by one then dozens
who batten on to the fruit, fluttering

in a flurry of excitement, white-eyed
with stabbing beaks quickly shredding
the plump figs to simple stalks.

Our tree, of course, and our figs.
Our wax-eyes, too, we like to claim
as if they owed us a living or something,

ungrateful tenants who scribble on
the wallpaper, smear and smudge the windows,
leave dog-turds on the lawn, eat our figs.

THE ONE-LEGGED BLACKBIRD

With one leg not two, he's a great little hopper.
He has to be. *Our knowledge can only be finite* says Popper,

a philosopher of whom this little black bopper
has possibly not heard, not even a whisper,

but Karl has a point, a legitimate view:
the bird can't imagine hopping on two.

From the path to the compost, the rail to the bin,
he's perfected the art of hopping on one,

a hop left then right, like a one-legged trooper
adroitly avoiding coming a cropper,

backwards and forwards, forwards and backwards:
thirteen ways for a blackbird to hop.

When destiny serves you a bad hand or rather a bad leg or rather a
    non-existent leg it may seem improper
but as mentioned *our knowledge can only be finite* says Popper:

when fate deals you an unfair cop,
there's nothing to do but to live in hop.

THUMPER

The cat was a bruiser,
a street fighter, a prowler
howling and yowling in the night.

He tore the sky to shreds
with ivory claws, his eyes,
two yellow moons, were bright
when Thumper did his rounds.

Such furry swagger, such contempt,
the real moon looked away quite cowed
then, cowled by gauzy cloud,
hid altogether. This squalling, brawling,
caterwauling, tight-balled hot shot
thought he'd lived forever. Should
have lived forever. He did not.

My husband is a reptile

1

Sometimes you have to take what you can get

It's not bad, really. He doesn't overheat at night so the sheets are always dry.

2

It could have been worse

He could have been a fish. I'm not fond of water in large quantities especially when it moves.

3

There are compensations

He's very easy to feed. He doesn't like cooked food and has no pining for sugary desserts. The house, too, is refreshingly clear of insects.

4

You have to take the rough with the smooth

I've grown to like his rough. There is a scaly tenderness about him. It more than makes up for the lack of conversation.

5

It takes all types

On occasions, I think I would prefer fingers, but toes are a reasonable substitute and have the added advantage of facilitating his crouching on the ceiling so that he is not under my feet all day and safely out of harm's way.

6

Notwithstanding

There are times I wish he were just a little less amphibian, a little more expressive.

7

But all things considered, better than nothing?

All things considered, better than nothing.

The **GRANITY**
Museum

THE GRANITY MUSEUM

I found my childhood
in the Granity Museum

before the rain fell
and the rain fell
and the hillside fell
all the way down the hill

my childhood
in a mason jar
the screw-top oxidised
the label washed away

across the road the surf
roared and the surf roared
like a mill saw and cut
the coast away

my childhood sat
static in a valve radio
flickered on a four-legged
black and white TV

the rain fell
and the trees fell
fissures split into
gullies of clay

my childhood squiggled
in mildewed music
teaching little
fingers to play

then while the rain fell
and the surf roared
my childhood
swept away

Four travellers in an Austin Maxi

They sang it in the navy-blue (or brown?) Austin as it climbed over the mountain.

They sang it on the white road through the gloom of the beech forest.

The white dust – or perhaps it was brown – billowed behind.

Sometimes I joined in: *O Veederzane! Sweetheart!*

A strange and haunting name, the promise of an impossible love, like Marlene, like Mercedes under a lamplight in European mist.

One traveller remembers a road littered with handbags, another antlered creatures in the trees, the third recalls the pink hot-water bottle growing cold, the fourth remembers an idea.

A girl named Goodbye. How many times did I dream of her before I said hello to you?

The sky would know. The blue sky – or perhaps the brown – the lost sky somewhere high above the dust.

MENSURATION

The road trip was measured
in miles, in kilometres,
Volkswagens, white horses
and signs saying falling debris.

The city trip was measured
in intersections, traffic lights,
Volkswagens, blossom trees,
and women on mopeds.

The car was full of obsessive
compulsives looking for
Volkswagens, green doors,
plates ending in 5, in 3,

something beginning with L:
letter boxes, laundromats,
lavatories, left-hand drives,
light bulbs, lorries, love.

And love? Love was measured
in telephone calls, clasped
hands and kisses, thunder,
lightning and falling debris.

Perhaps you should have kept your
hands on the wheel, your eyes
on the road, but you were
compelled elsewhere

needing something beginning,
or ending with love.

At Purau

A blue boat is said
to be unlucky,
for blue loves its own.

Yet this wedding party
walks along the jetty between
a rowboat guard of honour,

weathered pastel hulls
blue as the withered hills,
the washed-out sky.

In this water-colour world
so many blue boats
bobbing at their moorings;

a champagne moon rises
rippling silver in the late sun
and the sea becomes cobalt.

A yacht named *Moonlight*
is leaving the moonlight.
It sails into the darkness

a cargo of bride and groom
on board, hazarding fortune
on a wide black sea.

SHIP IN A BOTTLE

Why put a ship in a bottle?

He must have been sweet on Nancy
for he inked her name in loving capitals
onto the pennon he fixed to the mainmast,
the tiny pennon curved by an imagined wind.

How to put a ship in a bottle

1 Drink the whisky (Dewar's)
2 Lay down a choppy sea
3 Lift up a mackerel sky
4 Include a suggestive lighthouse
5 With delicate sails, fully rig the three masts
6 Smile mysteriously

His hopes

To place her under a painted sky
on a ship that can take her nowhere.

To join her there clutching the mizzen
just for'ard of the lighthouse where

they'll wait for the light that will never shine
near a bottleneck that will never open.

His rationale

She might have liked roses or forget-me-nots better,
although roses will fade and forget-me-nots wither
a little ship trapped in frozen weather will last forever.

A ship in a bottle, a metaphor, a mystery,
will last longer than flowers, longer than whisky,
longer than love, even longer than Nancy.

THE DRESSERS

The dressers have arrived in a white van to lay out the vacant house.

They have imagined a householder with dramatic eyeliner and a slash of lipstick sticky on her gash of a mouth.

She would have teetered on high heels crafted from dead crocodiles, her vermilion fingernails designed to pry and fetch the flesh of escargots from their shells.

To please her, the dressers have littered the rooms with shabby chic, with well-plumped pillows and cushions.

They have laid a table with settings for her three anorexic friends, decorating it with three large goblets designed in Pompeii, each stuffed with a stylised artichoke.

The artichokes do not look good enough to eat although they have been dusted with silver.

The dressers have thrown throws and crammed ironic vases with sprays of artificial flowers.

They have wrought iron and scattered rugs.

The dressers have left in a white van.

The house is mortified.

It waits, embarrassed, awkward, for the sound of a key in the door.

REFLUX

The mountaineers were confused. What could have caused it, this alpine burping? And all of them? Had their food been doctored, spam sabotaged, scroggin interfered with?

They were used to wind, but wind of the external kind, the wind that sculpted ice and rock, watered eyes and flapped jackets; this wind was something else.

External wind was dangerous, but the mountaineers could guard against it. They had ropes, belaying pins, gloves and goggles.

But this wind was internal wind and internal wind was equally dangerous: these chest heaves, these thoracic eruptions, could provoke a lurch, a clutch, a sudden spasm.

The mountain rose above their base camp, tall, cold and beautiful.

How could they face it now? How could they face its dangerous faces when what was solid could now shudder unexpectedly, could hiccough, eructate, cast them forth?

How could they face each other? Who could confess they had overlooked antacid? Who could forgive the mumbled excuses?

They could only decamp, unpitch their tents, hitch on their backpacks and make their way down the gentler, lower slopes, the backs of their hands to their mouths.

THE FUN DOCTOR

The Fun Dr stepped out of your diary leaving his phone number behind.

He had been given very bad advice: his suit was unsuitable. He should not have worn pinstripes, not with a pinstripe shirt (and not navy, not silver). The black tie was another miscalculation.

There were no spats. There was no violin case, although a number of lugubrious guitars did squeeze through the three speakers mounted on his cinderblock walls in sickly pallor, cream and pink.

He hadn't been in the game that long, he said, as if expecting the game to be over soon.

He was, he added, in need of a slogan, some point of difference beyond his cramped back room and plastic flowers, an age and a world away from Chicago.

An age, too, and a world away from viability, his bedside manner being insufficiently grave, almost as bad as his spelling. Somebody else had cornered *Dignity*, and another *Sincerity*.

He had thought of *Putting the FUN back in FUNERALS* but wasn't sure it had the right ring-a-ding.

DEACON BRODIE

And I saw that under the sun the race is not
to the swift, nor the battle to the strong …

– ECCLESIASTES 9:11

My watersider uncle arrives
with a bottle of over-proof
Deacon Brodie whisky especially
bottled for the Westport RSA.

Try it, he says, it'll put hairs on your chest.
Whether Deacon Brodie had
hairs on his chest, I am not aware
for while he bribed the hangman to let

him wear an iron collar on the morning
of his swinging, later that same morning
he was buried in unconsecrated
ground, so now we'll never know.

My uncle sits in the cab of the tallest
crane under the sun or rather the tallest
crane on the Westport waterfront
where his steel boom swipes at the sky.

This is as far as he can get vertically
from the tunnels of the mines where
sparrow fart each morning his four brothers
descend with their cribs and headlamps.

My uncle chain-smokes Melrose roll-your-owns
in order, he says, to make him cough
in order, he says, to clear his lungs.
Deep in the tunnels his four brothers

shovel darkness with wide, heavy banjos.
The brothers are as lean and muscled as he is
but cough just as much to clear *their* lungs
of the black dust that blackens everything.

Their strength, as they shift their tons of coal
and my uncle lifts his tons of cargo, I like to think,
is as the strength of ten, but whether their hearts
are pure must be at this point moot.

Deacon Brodie might have known this, being
an expert in what purity is and what purity
isn't, although again we'll never know because
of that hempen necktie which put an end to him.

However, whether their chests are pure is not
moot. Their coughing makes that quite clear.
And neither Deacon Brodie over-proof nor
chest hair, alas, can do anything at all about that.

And is the battle not to the strong? I guess that's
just wishful thinking, Deacon Brodie thinking.
My uncles have no opinion on this. They do lift
their shovels but are just as happy to lean on them.

The taxi driver searches for his daughter

He has a taxi driver's memory
crosshatched, a grid, graph paper.

He now knows the Knowledge
is linear, is streets, avenues,
pick-ups and delivery,
and quite inadequate.

His time is measured, metered;
his humour forced, his loss
as palpable and scratched
as a radio telephone.

She could have taken a left,
a right, or gone straight ahead.

She could be hiding in amber,
in scarlet, or in green,
or she may not be hiding at all.

She could be standing
in plain view like a plane tree:
her bark blotchy, holding aloft
her bright green leaves.

What she saw

She saw the handrail
of the bridge at the bottom
of her gully. She knew
she had to reach it, grip it,
lean over and retch.

She saw the road
stretching up the hill
with the gravel verge
blue with weed killer
and she saw poison.

She saw the two lines
outside the classroom:
girls boys girls boys,
the teacher's key chain:
its glint in the sun.

She saw the blackboard:
white black white black,
his chequered suit,
his soup-stained tie,
his rimless glasses
reflecting the sky.

VERTIGO

I'm not fond of the way you wobble, especially with the rocks so far below.
See how the waves smash upon them unpleasantly.

What's the matter with your middle ear, anyway? Is it set so that it defaults
to lurch? The path winds so narrowly, so tortuously,

and the spume flies like steam from an old loco, a loco that roars like the
ocean. Do you feel, falling, it would catch you tenderly

in its tender filled with soft coal for the boiler? Do you hope then that it
will chuggity chug your smudged self safely

away to some road broad and wide where you can wobble and lurch with
impunity? You're kidding yourself. Honestly,

there's no loco, only the rusted rails where it once shunted and they're as
hard as the kelp-covered rocks. Unforgivingly

they wait, sensing your distress. Close your eyes, lest you feel the urge to
ape the swaying kelp's example. I'll take your hand lovingly

and lead you home, past the tussock and the ice plant, down the steep
slope to where you can open your eyes again, and then gaze wonderingly

at the far horizon, where clouds spiral above as though a loco were
chugging there steadily, tranquilly, towards tomorrow.

THE BODY IN THE BED

It was there again last night
as it has been a number of times before:
the body in the bed, lying between us
or lying beside us, unmoving, peaceful.

It is the stillness and the peacefulness
I imagine that makes the body so unalarming;
it produces no anxiety, merely a mild curiosity,
rather like my curiosity about the nature
of the person who has stolen my slippers
or why the salt cellar happens to be in the fridge.

There is a mystery in its presence, too,
but a mystery similarly unthreatening.

Why this visitation, and why at this time?
Whose body is it, and why (and this may be
crucial) am I so aware of its presence
whereas I know it is quite unaware of mine.

Or, of yours, if it comes to that. I sense
it is unaware of you, even when you roll over
and move right through it to reach for me.

At these times it is almost comforting,
the body, me, you together in the bed.
Together until, in our deepening embrace,
the three of us become two,
the two of us become one.

SERENDIPITY

A happy accident when we met:
an unexpected corner turned
into a different landscape;

trees with heart-shaped leaves
(perhaps *catalpa*?); flowers I'd
not seen before, unusually coloured

(*coquelicot, sarcoline, amaranth*)
but oddly right; and in the shops
merchandise with foreign labels,

the exotic aroma of silks, of suks …
An unexpected corner and there you
were, where I knew you'd always been,

but familiar in a sudden moment,
stepping delicately into my memory,
making yourself comfortable

in a poppy-coloured chair.

PICNIC IN THE CEMETERY

Why the cemetery?

It was peaceful and there was plentiful parking.

What did you eat?

A boiled egg as white as the alabaster statuary I cracked it on.

Anything else?

Two cheese sandwiches washed down with a glass of Chablis.

You did not feel it was sacrilegious?

I did not think the dead would mind my continuing to eat.

What did you learn?

I was reminded of my impermanence; something I shared with the cheese sandwich.

What did you take with you?

The memory of cracking an egg on an angel.

LIFE AFTER THE DIAMOND HARBOUR FERRY

Under a mackerel sky the fish are hiding, porpoises sporting, and the ferry is trundling across the water.

The ferry is trundling across the wide water and we must cross the wide water in order to find our way home.

But the Diamond Harbour ferry finds trundling difficult. The passengers, the dogs, something it ingested is giving it indigestion.

We look at each other in alarm. Not even the white wake is comforting. There is an unspoken question in our minds: *Have we made our wills?*

The water is wide, the old song says. Will getting o'er require an oar? But there are no oars and the Diamond Harbour jetty looks miles away, hours away.

All at once the Diamond Harbour ferry burps, an eructation that sparks panic. Others have noticed. But the Diamond Harbour ferry does not apologise.

You take my hand and try to comfort me. *We must not allow our lives to be dominated by personification*, you whisper.

The jetty seems a little closer. Two black-backed gulls are perched on the railing. *She is quite right*, one screeches. *Listen to her.*

NOTES

'Letter to 'Oumuamua'. When it was detected by astronomers in 2017, 'Oumuamua was the first known interstellar object to pass through the solar system. There has been speculation that rather than an asteroid as first thought, or a comet as then suspected, 'Oumuamua may have been the product of an alien technology powered by solar sails. It was given the name *'oumuamua* from the Hawaiian language, meaning 'scout' or 'messenger'.

'Then Dr Salk'. Like almost all children of my generation I was given the vaccine for polio developed by Dr Jonas Salk in the early 1950s. Salk did not patent his vaccine as he wanted it to be freely available to the world. I received my oral dose in Aotearoa New Zealand in 1960 or 1961. As far as I know, there were very few sceptics or anti-vaxxers protesting at the rollout.

'We come easily to the language of horror'. Michelle Elvy, editor of *Flash Frontier*, challenged her fellow editors to write a piece of micro-fiction using as a title a phrase from an interview in the journal with Keri Hulme. I was allocated this title.

'The song of the forest at Marshalswick'. The Wick is a wooded park in Marshalswick, a suburb of St Albans, Hertfordshire, United Kingdom, and includes a remnant of ancient forest. The Charter of the Forest (Carta Foresta), agreed to by the young Henry III, was promulgated in 1217, just two years after its better-known companion the Magna Carta. The Charter of the Forest gave free men access to royal forests.

'Hoopsa boyaboy hoopsa!' was written in response to a challenge by Michelle Elvy and Marco Sonzogni, editors of *Breach of All Size* (The Cuba Press, 2022), to write a short piece to commemorate the hundred years since the publication of Joyce's *Ulysses* and the 1600th anniversary of Venice's founding in 421 AD. To make it tricky, those who accepted the challenge were given a phrase from the book and the stories had to be exactly 421 words long. My title came from Chapter 14. The two Venetians I knew most about were Marco Polo and Vivaldi. I plumped for Vivaldi.

'The coal range'. Auld Reekie (Old Smoky) is a nickname for Edinburgh.

'The complete lack of evidence is proof the conspiracy is working'. *Cui bono* is a Latin phrase meaning 'to whom is it a benefit?' or more succinctly 'who gains?'

'The Granity Museum'. Granity is a small settlement in the Buller district, north of Westport. Squeezed between the Tasman Sea and tall forested hills it is at risk from coastal erosion. The community museum was damaged by a slip after heavy rain in 2022.

'Four travellers in an Austin Maxi'. My parents used to like to sing a song called 'Auf Wiedersehen'. To my childish ears I thought they were singing about a girl named Veederzane.

'The Fun Doctor'. To her amusement my wife, Joan, discovered that, in her diary, she had abbreviated funeral director to fun dr.

'Deacon Brodie'. William Brodie, a highly respectable deacon or councillor in eighteenth-century Edinburgh, by trade a locksmith and cabinetmaker, spent his nights housebreaking, exploiting his knowledge of locks and keys. He was eventually caught, tried and, in 1788, hanged. It is likely that his double life inspired Robert Louis Stevenson's *Strange Case of Dr Jekyll and Mr Hyde*.

'The taxi driver searches for his daughter'. Acquiring the Knowledge (i.e. a memorisation of London streets, a formidable task) has long been a requirement for a licence to drive a London taxi.

ACKNOWLEDGEMENTS

My grateful thanks to my editor at home, Joan Melvyn, for her ever-astute readings of early drafts of these poems and for her honesty and unerring judgement, and to Anna Hodge, as always, for her exemplary final grooming of the work.

My thanks, too, to the members of my critique group (the Poots' Groop) namely John Alison, Marisa Capetta, Rose Collins, Diana Deans, Rodney Foster, David Gregory, Jan McAllum (Jan Hutchison), Frankie McMillan and Zoë Meager.

My thanks to the Canterbury Poets Collective and its committee for staging the Spring readings, where most of these poems were first aired before an audience.

I am grateful to the trustees of the Randell Cottage in Wellington for my six months in residence in 2018, when a number of the poems were first drafted.

I have many friends in poetry, too numerous to list, but for their support and encouragement I must make special mention of my editorial colleague Michelle Elvy, Michael Harlow, David Howard, Joanna Preston and Doc Drumheller. Thanks also to Mike Bartholomew-Biggs and Nancy Matson who arranged for a reading in the Crypt, St Mary's, Islington, London.

Special thanks to Sue Wootton, publisher at Otago University Press. I am grateful for her faith in this book and her care and enthusiasm in seeing it through.

My thanks to the editors of the following publications where some of these poems have previously appeared: *52/250 A Flash Year*; *Anima*; *Atlas*; *Bookends Review*; *Breach of All Size: Small stories on Ulysses, love and Venice*, edited by Michelle Elvy and Marco Sonzogni (The Cuba Press); *broadsheet*; *Catalyst*; *Cold Mountain Review*; *Crab Orchard Review*; *Delmarva Review*; *Dream Catcher*; *Faultline*; *Flash Frontier*; *Gargoyle*; *HCE Review*; *Landfall*; *London Grip*; *Love in a Time of Covid*, edited by Michelle Elvy and Witi Ihimaera; *New Flash Fiction Review*; the New Zealand Poet Laureate blog; *No Other Place to Stand: An anthology of climate change poetry from Aotearoa New Zealand*, edited by Jordan Hamel, Rebecca Hawkes, Erik Kennedy and essa ranapiri (Auckland University Press); *The Quick Brown Dog*; *Prole*; *Room to Write*, edited by Linda Burgess and Maggie Rainey-Smith (The Cuba Press); *Rhino*; *takahē*; and *Third Wednesday*.

Published by Otago University Press
Te Whare Tā o Te Wānanga o Ōtakou
533 Castle Street
Dunedin, New Zealand
university.press@otago.ac.nz
www.otago.ac.nz/press

First published 2023
Copyright © James Norcliffe
The moral rights of the author have been asserted.

ISBN 978-1-99-004851-7 (print)

Published with the assistance of Creative New Zealand

creative
nz
ARTS COUNCIL OF NEW ZEALAND TOI AOTEAROA

Editor: Anna Hodge
Cover image: Odilon Redon, *Guardian Spirit of the Waters*, 1878, charcoal and chalk on paper,
Wikimedia commons

Printed in Aotearoa New Zealand by Ligare.